The Bible of Bubbly

The Bible of Bubbly

Bartender's Book of Champagne Cocktails
with Recipes and Lore

by Michael Turback

DRINKS

INTRODUCTION

The story begins with Dom Pierre Pérignon, a Benedictine monk and cellar master at the Abby of Hautvil-
lers in the region above Epernay called Champagne.
Noting that local wines became fizzy during the second
fermentation each spring, he found a way to prevent
the bubbles from escaping. The wine we now call
Champagne is the result of the monk's labor and per-
sistence, including the art of mixing the fruit from different vineyards to achieve the perfect blend.

True Champagne is special because of its terroir –
the concept that great wines invariably express time
and place. Not only is Champagne specific to one
region in the entire world – a very specific area of less
than 80,000 acres in Champagne, France – but its com-
bination of chalky soils, easy drainage, and cool cli-
mate provide high acidity, low sugar, and a constant
stream of bubbles that trickle up the sides of the glass.

In order to safeguard their name, Champagne producers have signed agreements worldwide reserving
the name "Champagne" for wine produced in that
region and in that region alone. In the United States,
an agreement was signed banning use of
"Champagne" on domestic products but brands exist-
ing before 1986 were grandfathered in. Producers in
wine regions including Napa and Oregon have signed

agreements agreeing not to use the name Champagne, but some U.S. brands have continued to use the term generically. While sparkling wine is made throughout the world, there is only one true Champagne, and it's made in Champagne. Period.

There doesn't seem to be any point in drinking any other sparkling wine when there is something as distinctive and delicious as true Champagne. The most prestigious celebratory wine in the world, French Champagne has long been used as a means of ritual celebration at the coronation of Kings, launching of ships around the world, in literature, film, diplomacy, and pop culture. Journalist Edward Spencer Mott is the one who said, "'Tis an expensive restorative, no doubt; but Champagne – genuine Champagne – is about the most valuable restorative known to science."

Besides Mr. Mott, true Champagne has had countless devotees, white knights, and evangelists. American writer F. Scott Fitzgerald once commented, "Too much of anything is bad, but too much Champagne is just right." Poet and essayist Samuel Johnson wrote, "The feeling of friendship is like that of being comfortably filled with roast beef; love, like being enlivened with Champagne." French emperor Napoleon Bonaparte confessed, "I drink Champagne when I win, to celebrate, and I drink Champagne when I lose, to console myself." Dramatist, and diplomat Paul Claudel suggested, "In the little moment that remains to us between the crisis and the catastrophe, we may as well drink a glass of Champagne." "Why do I drink Champagne for breakfast?" asked Noel Coward. "Doesn't everyone?" "Pleasure without Champagne is purely artificial," insisted Oscar Wilde. In his later years, British economist John Maynard Keynes observed, "My only regret is that I have not drunk more Champagne in my life."

For Winston Churchill, "A single glass of Champagne imparts a feeling of exhilaration. The nerves are braced; the imagination is stirred; the wits become more nimble." During World War II, the British Prime Minister motivated the British forces with the exhortation, "Remember, gentlemen, it's not just France we are fighting for, it's Champagne!"

Certain women, it seems, have been very fond of Champagne. Madame de Pompadour, 18th century star of Parisian society who inspired the breast-shaped coupe glass, explained, "Champagne is the only wine that leaves a woman beautiful after drinking it." Other women have followed in her footsteps. Lilly Bollinger explained, "I drink it when I'm happy and when I'm sad. Sometimes I drink it when I'm alone. When I have company I consider it obligatory. I trifle with it if I'm not hungry and drink it when I am. Otherwise, I never touch it – unless I'm thirsty."

Bette Davis famously said, "There comes a time in every woman's life when the only thing that helps is a glass of Champagne." Coco Chanel insisted, "I only drink Champagne on two occasions, when I am in love and when I am not." "Champagne," explained Marlene Dietrich, "gives you the impression that every day is Sunday." Dorothy Parker wrote, "Three be the things I shall never attain: envy, content, and sufficient Champagne." Brigitte Bardot admitted, "Champagne is the one thing that gives me zest when I'm tired." Tallulah Bankhead sipped Champagne from her slipper, and Marilyn Monroe once took a bath in 350 bottles-worth of Champagne.

Billy Wilder's 1937 musical *The Champagne Waltz* was promoted as "gay and sparkling as a Champagne cocktail!" Victor Laszlo and Captain Renault both order Champagne Cocktails in the 1942 classic *Casablanca*, and Deborah Kerr and Cary Grant sip cocktails made with Champagne in *An Affair to Remember*.

Sometimes called "Chorus Girl's Milk," the Champagne Cocktail is elegant, timeless and delicious, and for over a century, bartenders have defied tradition and experimented with ways to add sparkle to mixed drinks. The following pages offer an eclectic collection of 88 tried-and-true recipes that explore the versatility of Champagne at the bar, from pre- and post-

Prohibition classics to inventive contemporary notions developed in progressive cocktail programs.

For you, dear reader, offered is a book's worth of inspiration and guidance. With this volume as trusted accomplice, you're invited to experience and appreciate, in the words of Charles Dickens, "one of the elegant extras in life."

CHAMPAGNE COCKTAILS

PRINCE OF WALES

The eldest son of Queen Victoria, Albert Edward (later to be King Edward VII), held the title of Prince of Wales for longer than any of his predecessors. With no official duties, Albert Edward was known as "the playboy prince," and typified the life of a wealthy late-Victorian gentleman of leisure. His biography, *The Private Life of King Edward VII*, credits the very first Champagne cocktail to the Prince himself, a recipe he passed along to bartender Jerry Thomas during an 1860 visit to New York.

> 1 basrspoon sugar
> 1 dash Angostura bitters
> 1 1/2 ounces rye whiskey
> 1 small piece pineapple
> 1/4 barspoon Maraschino liqueur
> Champagne, chilled

Stir together sugar and bitters in the bottom of a mixing glass. Add whiskey, Maraschino, and pineapple, and fill with crushed ice. Shake vigorously and strain into a coupe glass. Top up with Champagne.

BLACK VELVET

Brooks's Club in London was founded as a gathering place for London's most distinguished lords, barons and dukes. Legend has it that the Black Velvet was created by the club's bartender in 1861 to mourn the death of Queen Victoria's husband Prince Albert. The bartender thought the Champagne should also be in mourning, so he added Guinness to create an effect similar to the black armbands worn by the mourners.

> 4 ounces Champagne, chilled
> 2 ounces Guinness Extra Stout, chilled

Pour Champagne into a flute or other tall glass. Pour the Guinness on top. (Guinness is heavier. If you mix it the other way around, it won't combine evenly and will need to be stirred).

RITZ CHAMPAGNE COCKTAIL

Ah, the Ritz Bar, that society rendezvous just inside the discreet Rue Cambon entrance to the legendary hotel, appointed with red-velvet armchairs and Victorian furnishings, a marble fireplace and historic portraits. This is where the Champagne Cocktail hit its stride in the 1920s, attracting such notables as Ernest Hemingway, F. Scott Fitzgerald, and Cole Porter. Journalist Basil Woon reported that every morning at half-past seven Porter would leap out of bed, and arrange himself in a riding habit. Then, after writing a song or two, he would appear at the stroke of half-past twelve at the Ritz Bar, where he would say "Champagne Cocktail, please. Had a marvelous ride this morning!"

> 1 sugar cube
> 3 dashes Angostura bitters
> Champagne, chilled
> lemon peel

Place sugar cube in a coupe glass; soak with bitters. Top up with Champagne. Express lemon peel over the glass, rub it around the rim, and drop it in.

SAVOY CHAMPAGNE COCKTAIL

The American Bar at the Savoy Hotel was one of the earliest establishments to introduce American-style cocktails to Europe. Luckily for the Savoy faithful, the arrival of Prohibition forced barman Harry Craddock to flee New York's Knickerbocker Bar for the more permissive shores of England, although not before reputedly shaking the last legal cocktail to be served in the city. Once ensconced behind mahogany at the Savoy Bar, he added richness and gravitas to a glass of Champagne, a drink that furnishes visual stimulation, with fine bubbles flowing up from the fast-disappearing cube.

> 1 sugar cube
> 3 dashes Angostura bitters
> 1/2 ounce Cognac
> 1/2 ounce Grand Marnier
> Champagne, chilled
> orange peel

Place sugar cube in a coupe glass; soak with bitters. Add Cognac and Grand Marnier. Top up with Champagne. Express orange peel over the glass, rub it around the rim, and drop it in.

THE ALFONSO

Alfonso XIII, King of Spain, posthumous son of Alfonso XII of Spain, was proclaimed King at his birth. During his reign from 1886 to 1931 he was lovingly known as a dandy and a man who liked his Champagne in the bar at the Ritz beginning around noon. He was so fond of Champagne, bartenders of the Deauville Hotel in Normandy invented this cocktail in his honor.

>1 sugar cube
>4 dashes Angostura bitters
>1/2 ounce Dubonnet Red
>Champagne, chilled
>lemon peel

Place sugar cube in wine glass; soak with bitters. Add the Dubonnet and one ice cube. Top up with Champagne. Express lemon peel over the glass, rub it around the rim, and drop it in.

BOOTHBY COCKTAIL

He was a vaudeville jig-dancer, real estate agent, tailor, patent-medicine salesman, and, finally, a cocktail pioneer. While working as a bartender at the Silver Palace on Geary Street in San Francisco, William Thomas Boothby authored *Cocktail Boothby's American Bartender*, a bar manual containing novel cocktail recipes among the drinks, many gathered from other bartenders of the era. His own contribution was a self-titled, Manhattan-inspired Champagne cocktail.

>   2 ounces rye whiskey
>   1 ounce Italian vermouth
>   2 dashes orange bitters
>   2 dashes Angostura bitters
>   Champagne, chilled
>   Maraschino cherry

Combine whiskey, vermouth, and bitters in a mixing glass filled with cracked ice. Stir for 10 seconds and strain into a coupe glass. Top up with Champagne and garnish with a cherry.

FRENCH 75

Alec Waugh, author of *In Praise of Wine & Certain Noble Spirits*, calls the French 75 "the most powerful drink in the world." The name came from 75-mm howitzers placed along the Maginot Line during World War I, and much like the weapon, according to barman Harry Craddock of the London Savoy, the cocktail "hits with remarkable precision." Society journalist Lucius Beebe, who it is said could "drink a double bottle of Champagne without batting an eye," authored *The Stork Club Bar Book* in 1946, providing the club's recipe for "the celebrated French 75."

> 2 ounces dry gin
> juice of 1/2 lemon
> 1 barspoon powdered sugar
> Champagne, chilled

Combine gin, lemon juice, and sugar in a mixing glass filled with cracked ice. Shake vigorously and strain into a coupe. Top up with Champagne.

FRENCH 95

An American counterpart to the French 75, with bourbon replacing gin, and as a more appropriate companion to bourbon, orange becomes the dominant citrus. Crisp and bright and boozy, the drink is reminiscent of a carbonated Old Fashioned. The woodsy, spicy flavors of the bourbon are tempered by the bubbles of the sparkling wine.

> 1 1/2 ounces bourbon
> 1/2 ounce fresh lemon juice
> 1 ounce fresh orange juice
> 3/4 ounce simple syrup
> Champagne, chilled

Combine bourbon, fruit juices, and simple syrup to a mixing glass filled with cracked ice. Shake vigorously and strain into a coupe. Top up with Champagne.

FRENCH 125

Arnaud's French 75 Bar in the French Quarter of New Orleans, chooses to make its eponymous cocktail with Cognac in place of gin or bourbon, "in honour of the cocktail's French origins." Like the French 75, the cognac version was named after another gun, the tank-mounted Soviet 125-mm smoothbore cannon.

> 1 1/2 ounces Cognac
> 1/2 ounce fresh lemon juice
> 3/4 ounce simple syrup
> Champagne, chilled

Combine Cognac, lemon juice, and simple syrup to a mixing glass filled with cracked ice. Shake vigorously and strain into a coupe. Top up with Champagne.

JIMMIE ROOSEVELT

In 1939, Town and Country magazine sent Charles H. Baker Jr. on assignment around the world to find the very best food and drink. The result was *The Gentleman's Companion*, a grand cocktail tour that takes the reader on imaginative flights fueled by drinks like the Champagne Cocktail he christened after the oldest son of President Franklin D. Roosevelt. "It is cooling, refreshing, invigorating, a delight to the eye and palate," writes Baker.

> 1 lump sugar
> 5 dashes Angostura bitters
> 2 ounces Cognac
> Champagne, chilled
> 2 barspoons Green Chartreuse

Fill a 16-ounce thin crystal goblet with finely cracked ice. Saturate the sugar with bitters and place in the center. Add Cognac and top up with Champagne. Carefully float Chartreuse over the top.

BUCK'S FIZZ

"Champagne and orange juice is a great drink," explained Philip, Duke of Edinburgh. "The orange improves the Champagne, and the Champagne definitely improves the orange." In England, it's called a "Buck's Fizz," first poured in 1921 by Pat McGarry at the Buck's Club, the gentleman's club in London, as an excuse to begin drinking early. The formula of two parts orange juice to one part Champagne was reversed a few years later at the Ritz Bar in Paris, when barman Frank Meier composed one part orange juice to two parts Champagne for a drink he called the "Mimosa." While the more proper proportion is still debated, all agree the drink is improved with a dash of orange bitters.

>   2 ounces orange juice, freshly-squeezed
>   4 ounces Champagne, chilled
>   1 dash orange bitters

Pour orange juice into a flute glass. Top up with Champagne. Dash bitters over the top for aromatics.

SHE COULDN'T SAY NO

"Champagne is the ebullient ambassador with plenary powers at the Court of Ebriety," writes Crosby Gaige in his 1941 *Cocktail Guide and Ladies Companion*. He provides this rendering of the Champagne Cocktail as a "toast to the bride."

> juice of 1 lemon
> 1 ounce dry gin
> 1 barspoon sugar
> 5 dashes Angostura bitters
> Champagne, chilled

Combine ingredients in a mixing glass with cracked ice. Shake vigorously and strain into an 8-ounce highball glass over new ice. Top up with Champagne.

MIMOSA

Roots of the Mimosa, which sprouted a few short years after the Buck's Fizz, are said to reach the Ritz Bar in Paris, where barman Frank Meier went heavier on the Champagne and named the sparkling union after its similarity in color to a flower called Mimosa, favored by French gardeners. It is said the orange improves the wine, and the wine definitely improves the orange. (Meier later created an alternate version to the Mimosa, adding a splash of Apricot Brandy and calling it a Valencia).

    1 orange juice, freshly-squeezed and chilled
    Champagne, chilled

Fill a flute glass 1/3 full of orange juice. Top up with Champagne.

DEATH IN THE AFTERNOON

Ernest Hemingway is credited with creating this drink at Harry's New York Bar in Paris sometime during the 1930s after becoming a fan of Absinthe. The cocktail shares its name with the author's book, *Death in the Afternoon*, about the ceremony and traditions of Spanish bullfighting. His recipe was first shared in *So Red the Nose, or Breath in the Afternoon*, a cocktail book with contributions from famous authors. Hemingway's advice: "Drink three to five of these slowly."

 2 ounces Absinthe (or Pernod)
 Champagne, chilled

Add Absinthe to a coupe glass. Top up with Champagne.

IBF PICK-ME-UP

Members of the International Bar Flies (IBF), founded in 1924 by O. O. McIntyre at Harry's New York Bar in Paris, have included Ernest Hemingway, Scott Fitzgerald, George Gershwin, Sinclair Lewis, Franklin Roosevelt, Gene Kelly, Noel Coward, Thornton Wilder, Marlene Dietrich, and many more. Legendary bartender Harry McElhone created this communal eye-opener for an organization devoted to "the uplift and downfall of serious drinkers."

 2 ounces Cognac
 2 dashes Fernet-Branca
 2 dashes Cointreau
 Champagne, chilled

Combine Cognac, Fernet-Branca, and Cointreau in a mixing glass filled with cracked ice. Shake vigorously and strain into a white wine glass. Top up with Champagne.

CHAMPAGNE GLORIA SWANSON

Lucius Beebe (*The Stork Club Bar Book*) writes: "Glamourous and worldly Gloria Swanson, a celebrity unabashed in her tastes and determined on the best, likes to start the day with what, within the memory of the author used to have been known on the Continent as 'Kings Ruin,' because it was the traditional favorite of so many of the old, bearded kings of Europe who used to frequent Foyot's, the Cafe de Paris, Maxim's, and the Ritz in the days when the going for kings was good." The club served Miss Swanson's eponymous cocktail in a tall Tom Collins glass.

> 2 ounces Cognac
> Champagne, chilled
> lemon peel

Add Cognac to a tall glass half filled with ice. Top up with Champagne. Express lemon peel over the glass, rub it around the rim, and drop it in.

CHICAGO COCKTAIL

Chicago Sun-Times columnist Irv Kupcinet called Chez Paree "the most glamorous night club in history." Located on the city's Magnificent Mile, Chez Paree became Chicago's most famous watering hole as it emerged from the bootlegging and speakeasy scene of the 1920s. Patrons sipped the club's own Champagne Cocktail while being entertained by Nat King Cole, Louis Armstrong, Frank Sinatra, Tony Bennett, Bob Hope, Milton Berle, Carol Channing, Joey Bishop, Buddy Hackett, Jimmy Durante, Martin & Lewis, and Joe E. Lewis.

> 1 1/2 ounces brandy
> 3/4 ounce triple sec
> 1 dash Angostura bitters
> Champagne, chilled

Combine brandy, triple sec, and bitters in a mixing glass with cracked ice. Shake vigorously and strain into a chilled Champagne coupe glass. Top up with Champagne..

AIR MAIL

The first attempt at modern airmail was documented in 1911. It traveled from Petaluma to Santa Rosa, California and contained exactly three pieces of correspondence. The first instance of the Air Mail cocktail appeared in Esquire magazine's 1949 edition of *Handbook for Hosts*. It's not certain why the drink is named for the modern delivery method, but the Air Mail is a potent cross between the French 75 and the Honey Bee, with a splash of lime whisked into a turbulent mix of rum, honey and Champagne.

> 1 1/2 ounces rum
> 3/4 ounce lime juice, freshly-squeezed
> 1 barspoon honey syrup (2 to 1 honey & water)
> Champagne, chilled
> orange peel

Combine rum, lime juice and honey syrup in a mixing glass filled with cracked ice. Shake vigorously and strain over new ice in a Collins glass. Top with Champagne and add a straw. Express orange peel over the glass, rub it around the rim, and drop it in.

BELLINI

Opened by bartender Giuseppe Cipriani at Calle Vallaresso in Venice, Italy, in 1931, Harry's Bar has long been frequented by famous people, including Ernest Hemingway, Truman Capote, Maria Callas, Orson Welles, and Aristotle Onassis. The Bellini, invented by Mr. Cipriani sometime between 1934 and 1948, is named after 15th-century Venetian painter Giovanni Bellini. Thanks to Harry's international regulars, word of the refreshing drink quickly spread to Paris, where the drink was energized with the bubbles of Champagne.

> 1 barspoon peach puree
> Champagne, chilled

Pour peach puree into chilled flute, and gently add Champagne. Stir gently. Proper proportions call for one -third peach puree and two-thirds chilled sparkling wine (make sure to pour the puree into the glass first).

ILE DE FRANCE SPECIAL

The recipe for this "picker-upper" was passed along to Charles H. Baker by a habitual crosser on the Ile de France ocean liner. In *The Gentlemen's Companion* he recounts, "The bar maitre, one Reynauld, on this somewhat amazing craft has found that picker-uppers have to be even better than putter-downers the night before." And in tasting the drink, Mr. Baker notes, "the pungent herbs greet the nostrils, then the cool quenching of the viney bubbly."

> 1/2 barspoon powdered sugar
> 3/4 ounce Cognac
> Champagne, chilled
> 1 to 2 dashes Yellow Chartreuse

Add sugar and Cognac to a flute glass. Top up with Champagne. Use the back of a teaspoon to gently float Yellow Chartreuse on top.

KIR ROYALE

An apéritif of the Gallic persuasion, known originally as Blanc-Cassis, owes its present name to Felix Kir, hero of the French Resistance during the Second World War and Mayor of Dijon, who popularized the drink by offering it at receptions to visiting delegations. The French combine Champagne with Crème de Cassis for a more refined Kir Royale.

> 1/2 ounce crème de cassis
> Champagne, chilled
> lemon peel, cut into a finger-length strip

Pour Crème de Violette into a flute glass. Top up with Champagne. Express lemon peel over the glass and place it on the rim.

SARATOGA COCKTAIL

In Ian Fleming's novel, *Casino Royale*, James Bond called Harry's New York Bar the best place in Paris to get a "solid drink." The bar's founder, American jockey Tod Sloan, was so keen to recreate the atmosphere of a New York saloon that he had one dismantled and shipped to Paris. Sloane hired a Scots barman from Dundee named Harry MacElhone who eventually bought the bar in 1923 and renamed after himself. The Saratoga Cocktail is a Harry's original.

> 1 barspoon pineapple juice
> 2 dashes orange bitters
> 2 dashes Maraschino liqueur
> 1 ounce brandy
> 2 fresh strawberries

Combine pineapple juice, bitters, Maraschino, and brandy in a mixing glass filled with cracked ice. Shake vigorously and strain into a coupe glass. Top up with Champagne. Garnish with strawberries.

MONSIEUR CRESCENDO

Italian Composer Gioacchino Rossini's spirited and melodious Il Barbiere di Siviglia ("The Barber of Seville") is a piece of inspired inventiveness that has delighted opera lovers since it was introduced in 1816. Rossini arrived in Paris in 1823, he composed Il viaggio a Reims ("The Journey to Reims"), a cantata improvised for the coronation of Charles X. Parisians continue to honor him with a strawberry-red derivative of the Bellini, pretty to the eye and pleasing to the palate.

> 2 tablespoons puréed strawberries*
> Champagne, chilled
> 1 fresh strawberry, sliced

Place 2 tablespoons of puréed strawberries in a pre-chilled flute glass and top up with Champagne. Garnish with fresh strawberry on rim of the glass.

*In a bowl, combine 2/3 cup strawberries with 1 teaspoon sugar and 2 tablespoons Champagne. Using a fork, crush strawberries to a rough pulp. Place in refrigerator for 2 hours.

HELL AND
HIGH WATER

Ted Shane's Bar Guide was published by *True Magazine* and "dedicated to folks who value their lives, friends, futures, homes, and taste buds, and like to shake up a few for conviviality's sake." The drink may have been inspired by George Lippard's 19th century novel Empire City, in which a character is described as "wrapped up in an atmosphere of brandy and Champagne – on fire with the flames of alcohol – the very sublimest type of Satan in liquor."

> 2 ounces brandy
> 1 barspoon lemon juice, freshly-squeezed
> 1 barspoon grenadine syrup
> Champagne, chilled

Combine Brandy, lemon juice, and grenadine in a mixing glass with cracked ice. Shake vigorously and strain into a chilled Champagne coupe glass. Top up with Champagne.

PIMM'S FRANÇAIS

"England's gift to France is a potation made from dry gin, liqueur, fruit juices, and spices, invented in 1840 by a London oyster bar owner, and originally served as a healthful digestive aid. Tourists sip Pimm's and Champagne in beach bars along the French Riviera.

> 1 1/2 ounces Pimm's No. 1
> 1 slice orange
> 1 slice lemon
> 1 strawberry, quartered
> 1 slice English cucumber (lengthwise)
> Champagne, chilled
> mint sprig

Combine Pimm's, fruits, and cucumber in a highball glass filled with ice. Top up with Champagne. Garnish with mint.

SEELBACH COCKTAIL

The cocktail first rose to fame in the 1990s when bartender Adam Seger claimed to have discovered the recipe on an old menu from Louisville's Seelbach Hotel. The "forgotten" libation was said to have predated the Prohibition and had at one time been the hotel's signature drink. Twenty years later, Seger admitted he made up the whole story. The drink was his own invention.

> 1 ounce bourbon
> 1/2 ounce Cointreau
> 7 dashes Angostura bitters
> 7 dashes Peychaud's bitters
> Champagne, chilled
> lemon peel

Combine bourbon, Cointreau, and bitters in a mixing glass filled with cracked ice. Stir for 10 seconds and strain into a flute glass. Top up with Champagne. Express lemon peel over the glass, rub it around the rim, and drop it in.

ILSA'S BLUE DRESS

In a flashback scene in *Casablanca*, Rick (Humphrey Bogart) and Ilsa (Ingrid Bergman) are in Paris when the city falls to the Germans, and Ilsa is wearing a blue dress. She says she will only wear the dress again when the Germans leave Paris. Barman Kent Westmoreland of Windsor Court in New Orleans pays homage to this moment, transforming the traditional French 75 to pale blue with the addition of crème de violette. Vive la France!

> 2 ounces gin
> 3/4 ounce crème de violette
> juice of 1/2 lemon
> 1 barspoon powdered sugar
> Champagne, chilled

Combine Gin, lemon juice, and sugar to a mixing glass filled with cracked ice. Shake vigorously and strain into a coupe glass. Top up with Champagne.

VELVET SWING

Flamboyant 19th century architect Stanford White maintained a private lair on 24th Street in Manhattan where he entertained scantily clad chorus girls on a red velvet swing, hung from the ceiling with ivy-twined ropes. The story was told in *The Girl in the Red Velvet Swing*, a film starring Joan Collins, followed by the introduction of a red-hued Champagne Cocktail. Bartender Mikey Morrow's version is served at Toronto's Table 17.

> granulated sugar (to rim the glass)
> lemon wedge
> 1/2 ounce Port wine
> 1/4 ounce Cognac
> Champagne, chilled
> lemon peel

Spread sugar on a small plate. Rub the rim of a Champagne flute with the lemon wedge and dip rim in the sugar. Set aside. Add Port to a mixing glass with cracked ice and stir to chill. Strain into the prepared flute and top up with Champagne. Use the back of a teaspoon to gently float Cognac on top. Express lemon peel over the glass, wrap around a cocktail pick, and place at the edge of the flute.

THAI 75

The French 75 takes its name from an artillery weapon favored
by French troops due to its wicked fire power, a not-so-subtle
nod to the drink's lethalness. In Miami Beach, patrons of the
Khong River House are "transported" to an Asian street emporium
with flavors and traditions of the Northern Thailand region.
Khong's version of the classic cocktail softens the bite of Gin
with Lychee puree and binds ingredients with lemongrass syrup
to create fuller, more harmonious mouthfeel.

> 1 ounce gin
> 1/2 ounce lychee purée
> 1/2 ounce lemongrass simple syrup*
> Champagne, chilled
> lychee nut, speared

Combine gin, lychee puree, and simple syrup in a mixing
glass with cracked ice. Shake vigorously and strain into
a flute glass. Top up with Champagne and garnish with
speared lychee nut.

*Place 2 stalks of fresh lemongrass, 2 cups water, and 1
cup sugar in a saucepan and bring to a boil. Reduce
heat, and simmer, partially covered, for 15 minutes.
Strain the mixture and cool..

LE GENTLEMAN

The gentleman in question is Monsieur Jean Bud, whose family
had long been involved in the French wine region of Charente,
the birthplace of Cognac. In 1820, when he arrived in Italy, the
young Frenchman was fascinated by the quality of cultivated
vines in Romagna, between the upper Adriatic and Po Valley.
His legacy, Vecchia Romagna, adds virility to Champagne's
beautiful fountain of bubbles.

> 1 1/2 ounces brandy
> 1 ounce lemon juice, freshly-squeezed
> 1 barspoon brown sugar
> Champagne, chilled
> lemon peel, cut into a finger-length strip

Combine brandy, sugar and lemon juice in mixing glass
with cracked ice. Shake vigorously and strain into a flute
glass. Top up with Champagne. Express lemon peel
over the glass and place it on the rim.

HE WHISPERED IN HER EAR

Wood is a low-lit, low-key Chicago hangout where drinksmith Tommy J. Lansaw prepares a dry, herbaceous hybrid of a Martini and a Champagne Cocktail – glamorized with the bubbles and bouquet of Cava, the sparkling wine produced in Spain's Catalonia region.

1/4 ounce Chareau Aloe Vera Liqueur, for rinse
2 ounces Caorunn Scottish Gin
1/2 ounce Imbue "Petal & Thorn" Vermouth
2 drops organic thyme oil
Champagne, chilled
sprig of fresh Thyme, for garnish

Rinse a cocktail coupe glass with Aloe Vera Liqueur and discard the excess. In a mixing glass with cracked ice combine gin, vermouth, and thyme oil. Stir briskly and strain into the prepared glass. Top up with Champagne and garnish with thyme sprig .

EXCUSEZ-MOI

The French have a food and drink culture which lends itself well to the appreciation of complex spirits, with palates finely tuned and very perceptive to flavor subtleties. In a popular Parisian sipper, Scotch pairs brilliantly with Champagne, while a dash of Cointreau adds a bit of sweetness.

> 1 ounce Scotch whisky
> 1/4 ounce Cointreau
> Champagne, chilled
> Lemon peel, cut into a finger-length strip

Add Scotch and Cointreau to an Old Fashioned glass. Add one or two ice cubes and top up with Champagne. Stir gently with a swizzle stick. Express lemon peel over the glass and place it on the rim.

PURE POISON

Bartender asks a patron, "What's your Poison?" The answer at London's Salt Whisky Bar & Dining Room is a nimble, fruit-forward cocktail with rich textures and festive bubbles that play with a broad range of flavors. The hint of mint adds an aromatic nose to complement the sweet-tart potion.

>   1 ounce vodka
>   2/3 ounce Midori liqueur
>   1/3 ounce orgeat syrup
>   1/3 ounce lime juice, freshly-squeezed
>   1/4 slice of an apple
>   Champagne, chilled
>   fresh mint sprig

Muddle apple in a mixing glass, then add all ingredients (except Champagne) with cracked ice. Shake vigorously and strain into a red wine glass filled with crushed ice. Top up with Champagne. Garnish with mint sprig.

THE DAME

In *The Big Sleep*, as Philip Marlowe gets drawn into the affairs of the Sternwoods, the aged patriarch tells the shamus, "I used to like my brandy with Champagne – the Champagne as cold as Valley Forge and about a third of a glass of brandy beneath it." The suggestion is well taken by barkeeps Jared Meisler and Damian Windsor at The Roger Room in West Hollywood, California, with a Brandy-spiked sipper, sweetened and colorized with ruby-red cherry liqueur.

> 1 ounce Courvoisier VSOP
> 1/2 ounce Cherry Heering
> 1/4 ounce lemon juice, freshly-squeezed
> Champagne, chilled
> Maraschino cherry

Combine Cognac, Cherry Heering, and lemon juice in a mixing glass with cracked ice. Shake vigorously and strain into a chilled Champagne flute. Top up with Champagne and drop cherry into the glass.

PERLA ROSA

In this little pink number, Aperol adds a layer of subtle bitter orange nuance that mixes nicely with the botanicals of gin, while grapefruit juice provides a refreshingly tart twist. Champagne holds its own, keeping the drink zesty with effervescence while slightly softening the bitter flavors. To be enjoyed on its own or alongside traditional antipasti or sweets.

>3/4 ounce gin
>3/4 ounce Aperol
>3 ounces pink grapefruit juice, freshly-squeezed
>Champagne, chilled
>grapefruit peel, cut into a finger-length strip

Add gin, Aperol, and grapefruit juice to a Collins glass with ice. Top up with Champagne. Express grapefruit peel over the glass and place it on the rim.

NGUYEN DYNASTY

Named for the last ruling family of Vietnam, who defeated the Tay Son Dynasty, Jon Christiansen of Seattle's Ba Bar transforms the vintage Gin Fizz into a Champagne Cocktail designed to work in tandem with Chef Eric Banh's distinctive take on Vietnamese-inspired food.

> 1 ounce gin
> 3/4 ounce rhubarb syrup*
> 1/2 ounce lemon juice, freshly-squeezed
> Champagne, chilled
> star anise

Combine Gin, rhubarb syrup, and lemon juice in a mixing glass with cracked ice. Shake vigorously and double-strain into a chilled Champagne coupe glass. Top up with Champagne and drop star anise into the glass.

*In a small pot, combine 16 ounces diced rhubarb, 16 ounces sugar, and peels of lime and orange with 16 ounces water and bring to a boil. Reduce the heat to moderately low and simmer until slightly thickened and bright pink in color, about 20 minutes. Let the syrup cool then pour through a fine-mesh sieve set over a bowl. Press down gently and discard the solids. Add 1 ounce lemon juice and 1/2 ounce Vodka to preserve. Store in fridge until ready to use.

FAUX NEGRONI

The Negroni was invented in Florence in 1919. Half a century later, during what should have been the mixing of a standard Negroni at Bar Basso in Milan, Mirko Stocchetto reached for a bottle of gin, but instead picked up a bottle of Prosecco. This happy accident produced the "Bungled Negroni," a buoyantly bitter aperitivo. This version of the restrained, more easily quaffable drink bungled with Champagne.

    1 1/2 ounces Italian vermouth
    1 1/2 ounces Campari
    1 1/2 ounces Champagne, chilled
    orange slice

Build ingredients in a double rocks glass with ice, adding Champagne last. Garnish with orange slice.

FEMME FATALE

Bette Davis once said, "There comes a time in every woman's life when the only thing that helps is a glass of Champagne." Ms. Davis would surely approve of the vigilant mixologists at NoMa Social in New Rochelle, New York who embrace Champagne's flirtation with strawberries and sweet/tart lemon. Invite the girls over for brunch.

> 2 or 3 fresh strawberries + 1 additional for garnish
> 1 barspoon sugar
> 1 ounce Limoncello
> Champagne, chilled

Muddle fresh strawberries with sugar in a mixing glass. Fill with ice and add Limoncello. Shake vigorously and strain into a chilled Martini glass. Top up with Champagne. Garnish with strawberry.

MADHATTAN

If you've ever wondered if it's possible to improve on a master-piece, consider a French take on the classic Manhattan Cocktail. Rye partners with Amaro, the aromatic herbal liqueur, creating a swirling interplay of vanilla, citrus, licorice, cherry, chocolate and nutty notes – a full range of flavors animated with the vibrant personality of Champagne. It's dangerously simple to make, and the kind of drink that goes down very well after a big meal.

> 1 ounce rye whiskey
> 1/2 ounce Amaro
> 1 dash orange bitters
> Champagne, chilled
> orange peel, cut into a finger-length strip

Combine rye, vermouth, and bitters in a mixing glass filled with cracked ice. Stir gently, and strain into a coupe glass. Top up with Champagne. Express orange peel over the glass and place it on the rim.

MILLION DOLLAR DREAM

During the mid-1800s, British Army soldiers mixed black tea and rum in a drink they called "Gunfire." During the same period, Americans fortified tea with rum into Hot Toddies as prescription for chilly winter nights. At Rye on Market in Louisville, Kentucky, Bradley Hammond employs the historic fusion of tea and rum in an effervescent cocktail with a refreshing citrus finish.

1 ounce Plantation 3 Star Light Rum
1/2 ounce lime juice, freshly squeezed
1/2 ounce Earl Grey honey syrup*
2 dashes Bittermens Tiki Bitters
Champagne, chilled
lime peel

Combine rum, lime juice, honey syrup, and bitters in a mixing glass filled with cracked ice. Shake vigorously and strain into a coupe glass. Top up with Champagne. Express lime peel over the glass, rub it around the rim, and drop it in.

*Soak 1 teaspoon of loose leaf Earl Grey tea (or 1 tea bag) in 1 cup of warm water for an hour. Pour the tea into a saucepan and bring to the boil. Leave the bag/loose tea in the pan. Add 3 ounces honey and simmer for ten minutes. Remove from heat and double-strain into a clean (sterile) bottle.

THE MISTRESS

It's an industrial cathedral, crafted from the architectural arti-facts of the first power plant in downtown Los Angeles. The Edison's signature libation pays homage to the ascendency of the Champagne Cocktail in the 1920s with an adventurous varia-tion, electrified with Vodka, and amplified with luscious lemon and pomegranate. Prosecco provides the spark.

> 1 ounce vodka
> 1/2 ounce Limoncello
> 1 ounce pomegranate juice
> Champagne, chilled
> 1 fresh blackberry

Combine vodka, Limoncello, and pomegranate juice in a mixing glass filled with cracked ice. Shake vigorously and strain into a coupe glass. Top up with Champagne and drop blackberry into the glass.

NOCTURNE

Summer nights in the Cote d'Azur can be truly spectacular, especially when the full moon seems so close you can touch it. The early-evening drink has become a ritual in bars along the beach, where a sparkling confection with lovely ruby-red hue and hint of cassis speaks of the local passion for Champagne.

> 1/2 ounce vodka
> 1/2 ounce crème de cassis
> 1/2 ounce pomegranate juice
> Champagne, chilled
> lemon peel, cut into a finger-length strip

Combine vodka, crème de cassis, and pomegranate juice in a mixing glass filled with cracked ice. Stir gently, and strain into a flute glass. Top up with Champagne. Express lemon peel over the glass and place it on the rim.

DEAD MAN WALKING

The bar program at Levant, Scott Snyder's Arabesque restaurant in Portland, Oregon, is run by Abel Beazley, who revamps a French 75-inspired cocktail into a cultivated after-dinner refreshment, sweetened with liqueur made from Marasca cherries and deepened with bittersweet aromas of Italian digestivo.

1/4 ounce Campari, for rinse
3/4 ounce gin
1/2 ounce lemon juice, freshly-squeezed
1/2 ounce Maraschino liqueur
1/2 ounce Barolo Chinato
Champagne, chilled

Rinse a cocktail coupe glass with Campari and discard the excess. Combine the remaining ingredients (except Champagne) in a cocktail glass filled with cracked ice. Shake vigorously and strain into the prepared coupe. Top up with Champagne.

BROOKLYN BEE

Under the relentless guidance of Eric Ripert, Le Bernardin serves classically-rooted seafood cuisine at its most resplendent. This lavender- and honey-kissed cocktail with a splash of Champagne pairs effortlessly with Mr. Ripert's signature cooking.

> 1 3/4 ounces Brooklyn Gin
> 1 ounce lavender honey syrup*
> 1/2 ounce lemon juice, freshly squeezed
> Absinthe, for rinse
> Champagne, chilled
> lavender tea, for mist
> lavender sprig, for garnish

Rinse a coupe glass with absinthe and set aside. Combine the remaining ingredients (except Champagne) in a mixing glass filled with cracked ice. Shake vigorously and strain into the prepared glass. Top up with Champagne, and mist with a spritz of lavender tea. Garnish with lavender sprig.

*Steep 1/4 cup of dried lavender in 1 1/2 cups of near-boiling water for 15 minutes. Strain, measure the liquid and stir in an equal amount of honey. Let cool to room temperature, refrigerate and use within 2 weeks.

SANGRIA BLANCHE

Wine cocktails have long been mixed in the South of France, made-to-order at parties, cookouts, and other day-long summer extravaganzas. The tipples are meant to be enjoyed all day long in the sunshine. It's here that lush, fragrant peaches, nectarines and apricots combine with Champagne in an elevated sangria, served in large pitchers for passing around the table.

1 peach, pitted and sliced into wedges
1 nectarine, pitted and sliced into wedges
3 apricots, pitted and sliced into wedges
5 ounces peach brandy
1 cup peach nectar
1 750-ml bottle Champagne, chilled

In a pitcher, combine slices of peach, nectarine, and apricots. Stir in peach brandy and peach nectar. Just before serving, add Champagne, stir gently and add ice as needed.

SUDDEN
HEADACHE

At the sleek, candlelit bar of Chicago's Elm Street Liquors, guests order drinks from two menus, one geared to men (Pilsner list) and the other geared to women (the flute list). Sparkling cocktails from the flute list included the Margarita-inspired Sudden Headache.

>   1 1/2 ounces mango nectar
>   1 ounce tequila
>   3/4 ounce triple sec
>   3/4 ounce fresh lime juice
>   1/2 ounce simple syrup
>   Champagne, chilled

Combine mango nectar, tequila, triple sec, lime juice, and simple syrup in a mixing glass filled with cracked ice. Shake vigorously and strain into a flute glass. Top up with Champagne.

LADY GERMAIN

Chris Hannah is one of New Orleans' most beloved bartenders, manning the historic French 75 Bar attached to Arnaud's Restaurant, where he turns out impeccable cocktails with a reverence for the history that accompanies them. Mr. Hannah honors 18th century Lady Germain, a wealthy French aristocrat and courtier, with a Champagne potion, seasoned with strawberry and perfumed with elderflower blossoms.

> 1 ripe strawberry
> 1 1/4 ounces gin
> 1/4 ounce lemon juice, freshly squeezed
> 1/2 ounce St. Germain Elderflower Liqueur
> Champagne, chilled
> lemon peel

Muddle the strawberry in a mixing glass, fill with cracked ice and add the next three ingredients. Shake vigorously and double-strain into a flute glass. Top up with Champagne. Express lemon peel over the glass, rub it around the rim, and drop it in.

PERFECT THYMING

Commander's Palace, nestled in the heart of the tree-lined Garden District, is a New Orleans landmark that dates back to 1880. Born and raised in the Big Easy, bar chef Ferrel Dugas dresses her Champagne Cocktail to the nines with Bourbon, a splash of Praline Liqueur, and lemony aromatics of fresh thyme.

> 1 1/2 ounces bourbon
> 1/2 ounce praline liqueur
> 1/2 ounce lemon juice, freshly squeezed
> 1/2 ounce simple syrup
> 2 sprigs fresh lemon thyme
> Champagne, chilled

Muddle 1 sprig of thyme in a mixing glass. Fill with cracked ice and add the first four ingredients. Shake vigorously and double strain into a coupe glass. Top up with Champagne. Garnish with second spring of thyme.

LA STRATOSPHÈRE

French barmen pay homage to New York's Stork Club, where Nathaniel "Cookie" Cook and his crew invented dozens of drinks during the 1940s, including the sparkling Stratosphere cocktail with Crème de Violette and Champagne. The *homage français* includes Crème Yvette, a liqueur of violet petals and berries, the warming aroma of cloves, and native Champagne to create an after-dinner digestif.

> 3/4 ounce Crème Yvette
> 2 whole cloves
> Champagne, chilled
> lemon peel, cut into a finger-length strip

Add Crème Yvette and cloves to a flute. Top up with Champagne. Express lemon peel over the glass and place it on the rim.

MIDNIGHT IN PARIS

"Paris is always a good idea," said Audrey Hepburn. And from Geraldine, Toronto's Parisian-style bistro, Michael Mooney pays homage to the City of Lights with a Chartreuse-instilled, Absinthe-soaked libation, refreshed with cucumber, and animated with Champagne.

> 3 slices cucumber + 1 additional for garnish
> 1 ounce absinthe
> 1/2 ounce Yellow Chartreuse
> 3/4 ounce lime juice, freshly squeezed
> 1/2 ounce simple syrup
> Champagne, chilled

Muddle 3 slices of cucumber in the bottom of a mixing glass. Fill with cracked ice and add absinthe, Chartreuse, lime, and simple syrup. Shake vigorously and double-strain into a coupe glass. Top up with Champagne. Garnish with cucumber slice.

CIGARE CUBAIN

A sophisticated version of the Mojito created by Audrey Saunders at the Pegu Club in New York, the "Old Cuban" is both refined and refreshing, the drink combines tart and sweet with the spices of aged rum and adds the effervescence of Champagne. Bitters turn the drink the reddish-brown – the shade of a Cuban cigar – while bringing the complexity of flavors into sharp focus.

> 6 mint leaves (plus 2 more for garnish)
> 1 1/2 ounces Bacardí Añejo (or other aged rum)
> 3/4 ounce lime juice, freshly-squeezed
> 1 ounce simple syrup
> 2 dashes Angostura bitters
> Champagne, chilled

Add the mint leaves and simple syrup to the bottom of your mixing glass. Lightly muddle the mint in the simple syrup. Fill with cracked ice and add the lime juice, bitters and rum. Shake vigorously and strain into a coupe glass. Top up with Champagne. Garnish with 2 fresh mint leaves.

CATHERINE DENEUVE

Once pronounced the world's most beautiful woman, French cinema goddess Catherine Deneuve inspires a sparkling cocktail, created by mixologist Marcin Bilski at the Cellar Door, a quirky underground cocktail bar in Covent Garden, London. The clever pairing of Gin with fresh cucumber is first scented with elder-flowers and citrus, then animated with Champagne froth.

1 ounce Hendricks Gin
1/2 ounce fresh cucumber juice
1 dash lemon juice, freshly squeezed
1 dash Elderflower Cordial
1 dash simple syrup
Champagne, chilled
cucumber slice

Combine ingredients (except Champagne) in a mixing glass filled with cracked ice. Shake vigorously and strain into a flute glass. Top up with Champagne. Garnish with cucumber.

THREE NAKED LADIES

Morgan Nevans of Café Luxembourg brings a dash of glamour to New York's Upper West Side with a bubbly concoction named for the famous photo of three nudes standing at bar with their backs – and bare bottoms – to the camera. "We consider Absinthe, St. Germain and Champagne the 'ladies' of the cocktail," explains Mr. Nevans, "and always use true Champagne, not sparkling wine."

> 1/4 ounce Absinthe
> 1/2 ounce St. Germain Elderflower Liqueur
> 1/4 ounce lemon Juice, freshly squeezed
> Champagne, chilled
> lemon peel

Combine ingredients (except Champagne) in a mixing glass filled with cracked ice. Shake vigorously and strain into a flute glass. Top up with Champagne. Express lemon peel over the glass, rub it around the rim, and drop it in.

ATOMIC COCKTAIL

On January 27, 1951, the U.S. government detonated its first atomic device in an expanse of desert scarcely an hour's drive northwest of Las Vegas. Bars along the strip responded by creating a powerful concoction, popular in Las Vegas bars during the 1950s.

1 1/2 ounces vodka
1 1/2 ounces brandy
1 barspoon dry sherry
Champagne, chilled
orange peel

Combine vodka, brandy, and sherry in a mixing glass filled with cracked ice. Stir vigorously and strain into a coupe glass. Top up with Champagne. Express orange peel over the glass, rub it around the rim, and drop it in.

BEAUTY SCHOOL DROPOUT

It's a drink that is at once bright, citrusy and faintly floral.
Constructed by Krista Kemple at Decca Restaurant in Louisville,
Kentucky, the sparkling sipper borrows from multiple proto-
types in Champagne Cocktail history – spiked with an assertive
juniper spirit, tinged with aromatic bitters, and dolled up with
grapefruit essence.

> 1 1/2 ounces Junipero Gin
> 6 dashes of Peychaud's Bitters
> 1 ounce lemon juice, freshly squeezed
> 1 ounce simple syrup
> Champagne, chilled
> grapefruit peel

Combine ingredients (except Champagne) in a mixing
glass filled with cracked ice. Shake vigorously and strain
into a coupe glass. Top up with Champagne. Express
grapefruit peel over the glass, rub it around the rim, and
drop it in.

THE BLUR

"There comes a time in every woman's life when the only thing that helps is a glass of Champagne," Said Bette Davis. In this bubbly brunch cocktail from San Francisco's Nopa – meant to blur the lines between the night before and the morning after – Champagne enlivens the herbaceous Chartreuse, the mixture balanced with an eye-opening pour of tart lime juice and bitter-sweet, almond-flavored liqueur.

> 1 1/2 ounces Green Chartreuse
> 1 1/2 ounces Maraschino liqueur
> 1 1/2 ounces lime juice, freshly-squeezed
> Champagne, chilled

Combine Chartreuse, Maraschino, and lime juice in a mixing glass filled with cracked ice. Shake vigorously and strain into two flute glasses, dividing evenly. Top up each flute with Champagne.

MOOD INDIGO

"Music is the tonal reflection of beauty," said Duke Ellington, whose "Mood Indigo" is a textbook exercise in subtle sophistication. His introspective masterpiece, first recorded in 1930, has been a quintessential jazz/pop standard ever since. Its theme is reflected in the moody composition of apples, spices and herbs, amplified with Champagne.

> 1 1/2 ounces Calvados
> 1/4 ounces creme de cassis
> 1/4 ounces Green Chartreuse
> Champagne, chilled
> lemon peel

Combine liquid ingredients (except Champagne) in a mixing glass filled with cracked ice. Stir for 10 seconds and strain into a flute glass. Top up with Champagne. Express lemon peel over the glass, rub it around the rim, and discard.

AIDE MEMOIR

"Memory," wrote Oscar Wilde, "is the diary that we all carry about with us." Its name a play on aide-mémoire, French for a memory aid, a document that helps you remember something important, this formula from Jason Walsh of Bea in New York City is a balance of sweet and bitter with a float of Champagne for a celebratory air.

> 1 1/2 ounces Carpano Antica
> 1/2 ounce Yellow Chartreuse
> 1 dash orange bitters
> Champagne, chilled
> orange peel

Combine liquid ingredients (except Champagne) in a mixing glass filled with cracked ice. Shake vigorously and strain into a coupe glass. Top with Champagne. Express orange peel over the glass, rub it around the rim, and drop it in.

THE MAY QUEEN

The master chronicler of upper-class British buffoonery, P. G. Wodehouse's best-known contribution to the culture of drinking is his recipe from *Uncle Fred in the Springtime.* According to cocktail historian Scott C. Martin, the drink provides a sort of enhanced "Dutch courage" to its imbibers, inspiring them to propose marriage.

> 3/4 ounce brandy
> 3/4 ounce Armagnac
> 3/4 ounce Kümmel
> 3/4 ounce Yellow Chartreuse
> Champagne, chilled
> Guinness Extra Stout, chilled

Add brandy, Armagnac, Kümmel, and Yellow Chartreuse to a flute glass. Fill to 1/2-inch of the rim with Champagne. Top up with stout.

CORISTA

The vivacious Champagne Cocktail, once nicknamed "Chorus Girl's Milk," is among only a handful of drinks to stand the test of time despite minor adjustments in details of preparation. In this Italianized version from the Bar Ducale in Venice, Fernet-Branca adds color and gravitas to a glass of French sparkling wine .

> 1 sugar cube
> 2 dashes Fernet-Branca
> Champagne, chilled
> lemon peel

Place sugar cube in a coupe glass; soak with Fernet-Branca. Top up with Champagne. Express lemon peel over the glass, rub it around the rim, and drop it in.

THE BITTER SPARK

In this sparkling cocktail concocted by barman Jonny Almario at San Francisco's Hawthorn Lounge, Fernet-Branca makes a subtle appearance, just enough to provide drama without turning the drink into a liquid potpourri of herbal bitters. There are always sparks when putting two tyrants – Chartreuse and Fernet-Branca – in the same room.

1/2 ounce Fernet-Branca
1/2 ounce Chartreuse
1/2 ounce Amaro Montenegro
1/2 ounce Averna
Champagne, chilled
orange peel

Fill a coupe glass with ice and let it sit until the glass is chilled. Once the glass is chilled, toss the ice, pour in Fernet-Branca, swirl it around to fully coat the interior walls of the glass, then discard. Combine Chartreuse, Amaro Montenegro, and Averna in a mixing glass filled with cracked ice. Stir for 10 seconds and strain into the prepared glass. Top up with Champagne. Express orange peel over the glass, rub it around the rim, and drop it in.

OLD MONEY

Picture places of mahogany, red leather wingback chairs, and oriental rugs, where men of inherited wealth retire for cigars and cocktails. Drinks are strong and masculine, like this sparkling take on the classic Manhattan Cocktail. A barspoon of Fernet-Branca steals the show in partnership with the whiskey – a full range of flavors animated with the vibrant personality of Champagne. It's dangerously simple to make, and the kind of drink that goes down very well after a big meal.

> 1 1/2 ounces rye whiskey
> 1 barspoon Fernet-Branca
> 1 dash orange bitters
> Champagne, chilled
> orange peel, cut into a 2-inch strip

Combine rye and Fernet-Branca in a mixing glass filled with cracked ice. Stir for 10 seconds and strain into a coupe glass. Top up with Champagne. Express orange peel over the glass and place it on the rim.

NELSON'S BLOOD

 Admiral Horatio Nelson achieved some spectacular victories during the Napoleanic Wars, most notably the Battle of Trafalgar in 1805 where he was killed. is a champagne cocktail created from an unexpected mixture of champagne and tawny port, two entirely different derivations from standard wine. Nelson's Blood is named after Horatio Nelson, a famous British naval officer during the late 18th century.

> 1 ounce Tawny Port
> Champagne, chilled
> fresh mint leaves, for garnish

Add Port wine to a flute glass. Top up with Champagne. Garnish with mint leaves.

ORANGE BLOSSOM

Lively bubbles and delicate flavors give Champagne a transformative character that responds to subtle tweaks in a classic cocktail. Bitter plays against sweet as elderflower liqueur adds a lovely floral bloom. This elegant drink isn't meant to accompany food, but rather to tantalize the palate, paving the way for dinner. Not only modern, but *Français moderne.*

> 1 sugar cube
> 2 or 3 dashes orange bitters
> 1 ounce elderflower liqueur
> Champagne, chilled
> orange peel, cut into a finger-length strip

Soak sugar cube with the orange bitters. Drop the cube into a flute glass, add the elderflower liqueur, and slowly top up with Champagne. Express orange peel over the glass and place it on the rim.

SERENDIPITY

Colin Peter Field, chef du bar at the Ritz, created this cocktail for a regular client, a lover of Cuban cigars, specifically the Romeo y Julieta. When he served the gentleman the drink, the man said "serendipity!" According to Colin, Serendipity is a tribute to the Normandy region where they have always made apple brandy. "When you smell the drink, you smell apples, but you also smell the earth. It's France in a glass."

> 1 ounce apple brandy
> fresh mint sprig
> 1 ounce apple juice
> Champagne, chilled

Add apple brandy to a tumbler with the mint and muddle together, slightly bruising the mint. Fill with ice and add the apple juice. Top up with Champagne.

OLD HAT

This long-ago "pick-me-up" was once en vogue with a loose affil-
iation of drinkers called the International Bar Flies, whose home
base was Harry's New York Bar in Paris. In this riff on the original, Cointreau adds a cozy, orangey warmth to the bubbles of
Champagne, and Fernet-Branca crowns the drink with a layer
of bitter, herbal savor.

> 1 1/2 ounces Cointreau
> Champagne, chilled
> 1 barspoon Fernet-Branca
> orange peel

Pour Cointreau into a flute glass. Top up with Champagne. Hold a spoon directly over the drink, rounded
side up, and gently pour Fernet-Branca over the spoon,
creating a "float" on top of the drink. Express orange
peel over the glass, rub it around the rim, then discard.

MAZARINETTE

This is the signature cocktail of the Prescription Cocktail Club at 23 Rue Mazarine in Paris, where guests order drinks from the vest-wearing barkeeps and socialize amidst the elegant and modish décor of antique table lamps, dim lighting, Japanese crane wallpaper, and a long marble bar. The name refers to the seven nieces of Jules Mazarin, Chief Minister of France during the reign of King Louis XIV.

> 1 barspoon lemon juice, freshly-squeezed
> 1 tablespoon rhubarb juice*
> 1 ounce sloe gin
> 3/4 ounce gin
> 1 ounce Sipsmith Summer Cup aperitif
> Champagne, chilled

Combine lemon juice, rhubarb juice, sloe gin, gin, and Summer Cup in a mixing glass filled with cracked ice. Shake vigorously and strain into a Martini glass. Top up with Champagne.

*Chop one bunch of fresh rhubarb into ¾-inch pieces. Cover with water and simmer for about 30 minutes. Strain through a mesh and allow to cool. Refrigerate until ready to use.

FLIRTINI

A Martini only by a long stretch of the imagination, this iconic drink was developed for Sex and the City actress Sarah Jessica Parker by a bartender at Guastavino's in New York City. This pink, fruity, feminine drink is most often mixed for a girls-night-in or bachelorlette party.

> 1 ounces vodka
> 2 ounces pineapple juice
> Champagne, chilled

Combine vodka and pineapple juice in a mixing glass filled with cracked ice. Shake vigorously and strain into a Martini glass. Top up with Champagne.

ARISE MY LOVE

The drink takes its name from the 1940 film starring Claudette Colbert as a fashion reporter who is tired of writing about clothes while in France in the days leading up to World War II. She decides to write a real story for once, as World War II breaks out. The classic green minty Champagne cocktail is also known as the Emerald Gem cocktail.

> 1 barspoon green crème de menthe
> Champagne, chilled

Add crème de menthe to a flute glass. Top up with Champagne.

LA FÊTE

Baccarat is synonymous with French luxury and crystal crafts-manship, and its flagship luxury hotel is located in Manhattan. The bar's resident mixologist, Matthieu Yamoum, serves his signature Champagne cocktail in stunning pieces of Baccarat crystal.

> 1 ounce pineapple rum
> 1/2 ounce vanilla syrup*
> 1/2 ounce passion fruit puree
> Champagne, chilled
> lime wedge

Combine pineapple rum, vanilla syrup, and passion fruit puree in a mixing glass filled with cracked ice. Shake vigorously and strain into a flute glass. Top up with Champagne.

*Mix 1 1/2 teaspoons vanilla extract into 1 cup simple syrup (made with equal parts water and sugar).

CONTRAIRE

Vermouth originated in the ancient Duchy of Savoy, which covered parts of northern Italy and southern France, as winemakers added herbs and spices to improve the flavor of the region's then-inferior wines. The first branded vermouth was a sweet red variety made by Antonio Carpano in Turin, Italy, in 1786; 14 years later, Joseph Noilly introduced the first French dry version in the village of Marseillan. The marriage of *Italiano e Francese* creates layers of complexity, wrapped in the bubbles of Champagne.

> 1 1/2 ounces Italian vermouth
> 1 1/2 ounces French vermouth
> Champagne, chilled
> lemon peel, cut into a finger-length strip

Fill a large wine goblet with ice cubes. Add both vermouths, then top up with Champagne. Express lemon peel over the glass and place it on the rim.

BENEDICTION

St. Benedict established monasteries in Italy, and legend has it that Dom Bernado Vincelli, a Venetian Benedictine monk, first combined a medicinal elixir of 27 herbs and spices while visiting the abbey of Fécamp in Normandy, France. A wine merchant by the name of Alexandre Le Grand appropriated the formula to produce a liqueur he called Bénédictine. A dash of bitters is crucial to the marriage of Bénédictine and Champagne.

> 3/4 ounce Bénédictine
> Champagne, chilled
> 1 dash Orange Bitters

Pour Bénédictine into a flute glass. Top up with Champagne. Dash bitters over the top for aromatics.

LE TAUREAU

Ernest Hemingway held a lifelong fascination for French culture and cuisine. He first visited France during World War I as an ambulance driver for the Red Cross, and throughout the rest of his life he was drawn back to Paris where he wrote stories and drank wine (and it was good). A variation of Hemingway's Death in the Afternoon, his cocktail creation (and also the name of his book about the ceremony and tradition of Spanish bull-fighting) is the potent pairing of absinthe and Champagne.

    1 1/2 ounces Absinthe
    Champagne, chilled

Pour absinthe into a flute glass. Slowly add Champagne until a milky cloud appears.

OLIVETO

The olive tree is one of the defining features of Italy's land-scape, and its fruit symbolizes life, renewal, resilience, and peace. Olive brine adds tangy complexity to bittersweet notes of Amaro and the soft citrus scents of Aperol in a serendipitous partnership with French Champagne. Each sip awakens the pal-ate and stimulates the appetite for an evening of good food and good cheer.

        1 ounce Amaro Averna
        1/4 ounce Aperol
        1/2 ounce olive brine
        1 green olive*
        Champagne, chilled
        orange slice

Pour Amaro, Aperol, olive juice and olive into a flute glass. Top up with Champagne. Garnish with orange slice.

*To fully appreciate the drink, use a Sicilian Castelvetra-no olive, unique for its bright hue, buttery, sweet flavor and meaty texture.

CESAR RITZ

He was known as "king of hoteliers" and "hotelier to kings," and it is from his name and that of his hotels that the term "ritzy" derives. Cesar Ritz created the concept of the "grand hotel," most famously as founder of the Hôtel Ritz in Paris and the Ritz Hotel in London. The Rivoli Bar in London serves this cocktail in his honor.

> 1 ounce Armagnac
> 3/4 ounce peach liqueur
> 1/2 ounce grenadine
> Champagne, chilled

Combine Armagnac, peach liqueur, and grenadine in a mixing glass filled with cracked ice. Shake vigorously and strain into a flute glass. Top up with Champagne.

ASCENSION

At Drink, the craft cocktail lounge in the Fort Point section of South Boston, customers sip cocktails from unique vintage glasses and mugs. The sparkling Ascension, created by bartender Ren Brown for one of Drink's favorite regulars, balances a bit of warming spice with a bitter backbone.

> 1/2 ounce allspice dram
> 1/4 ounce Campari
> 1 ounce absinthe
> Champagne, chilled

Pour allspice dram into a chilled flute. Slowly pour in the Campari, followed by the Champagne, and top with a layer of absinthe.

AMOUR DU BALICO

The French sometimes call basil l'herbe royale (royal herb). In earlier times, when a woman wore a sprig of basil in her hair, it was a sign that she was looking for love, while a man would place a sprig of basil in his hair in an attempt to win a woman's heart. Today, the sweet perfume of basil is not only a staple of cooking in Provence, it teams with lemon in a sparkling, low-alcohol cocktail that's popular with residents in the Nice region.

> 1 1/2 ounces basil simple syrup*
> 1 barspoon lemon juice, freshly-squeezed
> Champagne, chilled
> fresh basil sprig

Add the simple syrup and lemon juice to a flute glass. Top up with Champagne. Garnish with basil sprig.

*Stir together 1 cup sugar, 1 cup water, and 1 cup loosely-packed fresh basil in a medium saucepan over medium-high heat. Bring to a boil, stirring occasionally, and boil 1 minute or until sugar is dissolved. Remove from heat, and let stand 30 minutes. Pour liquid through a wire-mesh strainer into an airtight container, discarding basil. Refrigerate until ready to use.

COCKTAIL 228

Guests at Hotel Le Meurice, located between Place de la Concorde and the Louvre, have included Franklin D. Roosevelt, Wilbur Wright, Salvador Dalí, and Rudyard Kipling. Bar director, William Oliveri created Cocktail 228, in honor of the famous Parisian bar and the 5-star hotel's historic address on Rue de Rivoli. Relax on leather armchairs surrounded by dark woodwork furnishings and sip Champagne cocktails with kings, sultans, and other eminent guests.

1 barspoon pear puree
1/2 ounce pear liqueur
1/2 ounce lychee liqueur
1/2 barspoon raspberry puree

Combine pear coulis, pear liqueur, lychee liqueur, and raspberry coulis in a mixing glass filled with cracked ice. Shake vigorously and strain into a flute glass. Top up with Champagne.

SPARKLING AMERICANO

Dating back to the 1860s, the thirst quencher was originally called "Milano-Turino," for Milan and Turin, home cities of its primary ingredients, and first served at Caffé Camparino. During Prohibition the Italians dubbed it the "Americano" for its popularity among American expats. The spicy, herbal, and distinctively bitter character of Campari (known as the "Red Mistress") radiates as Champagne replaces soda water of the classic.

> 1 ounce Campari
> 1 ounce Italian vermouth
> Champagne, chilled
> orange slice

Pour Campari and vermouth into a rocks or highball glass filled with ice. Add a splash of Champagne and garnish with orange slice.

FERNET ME NOT

At London's Callooh Callay Bar, named for Lewis Carroll's Jab-
berwocky, drinksmith Terry Cashman reimagines the classic
Southside Fizz with cucumber in place of fresh mint and Champagne subbing in for club soda. A modest measure of Fernet-
Branca adds another layer of flavor and complexity without
overpowering the drink.

> 1 slice cucumber, muddled
> 2/3 ounce simple syrup
> 2/3 ounce gin
> 1/3 ounce Fernet-Branca
> 1/3 ounce lemon juice
> Champagne, chilled

Combine ingredients (except Champagne) in a mixing
glass filled with cracked ice. Shake vigorously, then use
a hawthorne strainer and a fine mesh strainer to filter the
contents into a chilled cocktail coupe. Top up with
Champagne.

SOUTHSIDE ROYALE

The Southside Cocktail was created in New York City at the 21 Club, which was originally a speakeasy during Prohibition named "Jack and Charlie's" after its two owners. A tall cooling drink of gin, lemon juice, sugar, mint and soda, the Southside has been a particular privilege of the privileged class. Variations include this sparkling version.

> 2 ounces gin
> 3/4 ounce simple syrup
> 3/4 ounce fresh lime juice
> Champagne, chilled
> sprig of fresh mint

Combine gin, simple syrup and lime juice in a mixing glass filled with cracked ice. Top up with Champagne. Garnish with mint sprig.

TIZIANO

Harry's Bar in Venice is a cultural institution. When founder Giuseppe Cipriani opened the doors in 1931, the place became a favorite of almost every famous name to visit Venice, including Charlie Chaplin, Orson Welles, and Ernest Hemingway. The Tiziano, a variant of the bar's signature Bellini, was devised by Mr. Cipriani in 1948.

> 2 ounces red grape juice, chilled
> Champagne, chilled
> 1 red grape, skewered

Add grape juice to a flute glass. Top up with Champagne. Garnish with skewered grape.

DARLING LILLET

A light, breezy apéritif, Lillet is made from Sauvignon Blanc and Semillon grapes with macerated fruit liqueurs, providing a pleasantly fruity, but not overly sweet character. Its intoxicating perfume mixed with lemon verbena is almost spellbinding, and as Champagne mingles floral and fruit notes, the drink becomes pure magic.

> 1 ounce Lillet Blanc
> 2 tablespoons lemon verbena syrup*
> Champagne, chilled
> orange peel, cut into a finger-length strip

Add the Lillet and verbena syrup to a coupe glass. Top up with Champagne. Express orange peel over the glass and place it on the rim.

*Combine 1 cup sugar and 1 cup water in a small saucepan. Heat to boiling. Cook until the syrup is clear and the sugar is dissolved. Remove the syrup from the heat and stir in 2 tablespoons of dried lemon verbena leaves or 1 large fresh leaf. Let stand and steep 20 to 30 minutes. Strain and chill.

CHAMPAGNE SIDECAR

Originally published in 1937 by the United Kingdom Bartenders Guild, *The Café Royal Cocktail Book* compiled by William J. Tarling, head bartender at the Café Royal, offered a rare glimpse into the wide array of drinks offered in London bars between the two world wars. Notable among the offerings was this festive take on the classic Sidecar cocktail.

> 1/2 ounce lemon juice, freshly-squeezed
> 1/2 ounce Cointreau
> 1/2 ounce brandy
> Champagne, chilled

Combine lemon juice, Cointreau, and brandy in a mixing glass filled with cracked ice. Shake vigorously and strain into a coupe glass. Top up with Champagne.

CHANEL NO. 6

Working as a singer in a French caberet, Gabrielle Chanel acquired the name "Coco" from a popular song of the early 1900s, and she went on to change the course of fashion history. In her words, "I only drink Champagne on two occasions: when I'm in love and when I'm not." Bar Hemingway at the Ritz Hotel created this drink in her honor.

3/4 ounce vodka
3/4 ounce Chambord
3/4 ounce chilled pineapple juice
Champagne, chilled
fresh raspberry

Combine vodka, Chambord, and pineapple juice in a mixing glass filled with cracked ice. Shake vigorously and strain into a flute glass. Top up with Champagne. Garnish with raspberry.

DIABOLITAN

The origin of the original Cosmopolitan cocktail is disputed, most likely created independently by different bartenders since the 1970s. It was further popularized among young women by its frequent mention on the television program *Sex and the City*, where Sarah Jessica Parker's character, Carrie Bradshaw, commonly ordered the drink when out with her girlfriends. Variations include this sparkling version.

> 1/2 ounce Cointreau
> 1/2 ounce lime juice, freshly-squeezed
> 1/2 ounce cranberry juice
> 1 ounce vodka
> Champagne, chilled

Combine Cointreau, lime juice, cranberry juice, and vodka in a mixing glass filled with cracked ice. Shake vigorously and strain into a flute glass. Top up with Champagne.

FRENCH KISS

This tradition, which normally involves planting an air kiss on each cheek (sometimes up to four times depending on where in France you are). Local legend says that lovers are granted eternal love and bliss if they kiss on the Pont Marie bridge which crosses the Seine in Paris. In this popular confection, served in bars along the Left Bank, elderflower adds a subtle, sweet undertone to the generous bubbles of Champagne..

1 barspoon granulated sugar (to rim the glass)
1 ounce gin
1/2 ounce St. Germain Elderflower Liqueur
Champagne, chilled

Place sugar on a small plate. Run a lime wedge around the rim of a flute glass and press the rim of the glass in the sugar to coat. Add gin and elderflower liqueur to the prepared glass. Top up with Champagne.

THE MOONWALK

Joe Gilmore, legendary Head Barman at the Savoy Hotel's American Bar, invented this "giant leap" of a cocktail in 1969 to commemorate the first moon landing. The drink was the first thing astronauts Neil Armstrong and Buzz Aldrin sipped upon returning to earth.

> 1 ounce fresh grapefruit juice
> 1 ounce Grand Marnier
> 3 drops rose water
> Champagne, chilled

Combine grapefruit juice, Grand Marnier, and rose water in a mixing glass filled with cracked ice. Shake vigorously and strain into a flute glass. Top up with Champagne.

A FEW PAGES
FOR YOUR
OWN RECIPES

COPYRIGHT NOTICE

History Company LLC
www.historycompany.com
(800) 891-0466

Printed in the United States of America

CPSIA information can be obtained
at www.ICGtesting.com
Printed in the USA
FSHW011905241120
76267FS